MEXICO
BEAUTIFUL LAND
DIVERSE PEOPLE

THE PEOPLE OF MEXICO

COLLEEN MADONNA FLOOD WILLIAMS

This statue, found on the Yucatán Peninsula, depicts Chac Mool—an intermediary between the human and divine world. The Maya people would place offerings to the gods on the statue's stomach.

MEXICO
BEAUTIFUL LAND
DIVERSE PEOPLE

THE PEOPLE
OF MEXICO

COLLEEN MADONNA FLOOD WILLIAMS

Mason Crest Publishers
Philadelphia

Produced by OTTN Publishing, Stockton, N.J.

Mason Crest Publishers
370 Reed Road
Broomall PA 19008
www.masoncrest.com

First printing

1 3 5 7 9 8 6 4 2

Library of Congress Cataloging-in-Publication Data

   Williams, Colleen Madonna Flood.
    The people of Mexico / Colleen Madonna Flood Williams.
       p. cm. — (Mexico—beautiful land, diverse people)
    ISBN 978-1-4222-0663-8 (hardcover) — ISBN 978-1-4222-0730-7 (pbk.)
    1. Indians of Mexico—History—Juvenile literature. 2. Indians of Mexico—Social life and customs—Juvenile literature. I. Title.
    F1219.W55 2008
    972.00'497—dc22
                           2008031861

TABLE OF CONTENTS

MEXICO
BEAUTIFUL LAND
DIVERSE PEOPLE

INTRODUCTION

Mexico is a country in the midst of great change. And what happens in Mexico reverberates in the United States, its neighbor to the north.

For outsiders, the most obvious of Mexico's recent changes has occurred in the political realm. From 1929 until the end of the 20th century, the country was ruled by a single political party: the Partido Revolucionario Institucional, or PRI (in English, the Institutional Revolutionary Party). Over the years, PRI governments became notorious for corruption, and the Mexican economy languished. In 2000, however, the PRI's stranglehold on national politics was broken with the election of Vicente Fox as Mexico's president. Fox, of the Partido de Acción Nacional (National Action Party), or PAN, promised political reform and economic development but had a mixed record as president. However, another PAN candidate, Felipe Calderón, succeeded Fox in 2006 after a hotly contested and highly controversial election. That election saw Calderón win by the slimmest of margins over a candidate from the Partido de la Revolución Democrática (Party of the Democratic Revolution). The days of one-party rule in Mexico, it seems, are gone for good.

Mexico's economy, like its politics, has seen significant changes in recent years. A 1994 free-trade agreement with the United States and Canada, along with the increasing transfer of industries from government control to private ownership under President Fox and President Calderón, has helped spur economic growth in Mexico. When all the world's countries are compared,

Mexico now falls into the upper-middle range in per-capita income. This means that, on average, Mexicans enjoy a higher standard of living than people in the majority of the world's countries. Yet averages can be misleading. In Mexico there is an enormous gap between haves and have-nots. According to some estimates, 40 percent of the country's more than 100 million people live in poverty. In some areas of Mexico, particularly in rural villages, jobs are almost nonexistent. This has driven millions of Mexicans to immigrate to the United States (with or without proper documentation) in search of a better life.

By 2006 more than 11 million people born in Mexico were living in the United States (including more than 6 million illegal immigrants), according to estimates based on data from the Pew Hispanic Center and the U.S. Census Bureau. Meanwhile, nearly one of every 10 people living in the United States was of Mexican ancestry. Clearly, Mexico and Mexicans have had—and will continue to have—a major influence on American society.

It is especially unfortunate, then, that many American students know little about their country's neighbor to the south. The books in the MEXICO: BEAUTIFUL LAND, DIVERSE PEOPLE series are designed to help correct that.

As readers will discover, Mexico boasts a rich, vibrant culture that is a blend of indigenous and European—especially Spanish—influences. More than 3,000 years ago, the Olmec people created a complex society and built imposing monuments that survive to this day in the Mexican states of Tabasco and Veracruz. In the fifth century A.D., when the Roman Empire collapsed and Europe entered its so-called Dark Age, the Mayan civilization was already flourishing in the jungles of the Yucatán Peninsula—and it would enjoy another four centuries of tremendous cultural achievements. By the time the Spanish conqueror Hernán Cortés landed at Veracruz in 1519, another great indigenous civilization, the Aztecs, had emerged to dominate much of Mexico.

With a force of about 500 soldiers, plus a few horses and cannons, Cortés marched inland toward the Aztec capital, Tenochtitlán. Built in the middle of a lake in what is now Mexico City, Tenochtitlán was an engineering marvel and one of the largest cities anywhere in the world at the time. With allies from among the indigenous peoples who resented being ruled by the Aztecs—and aided by a smallpox epidemic—Cortés and the Spaniards managed to conquer the Aztec Empire in 1521 after a brutal fight that devastated Tenochtitlán.

It was in that destruction that modern Mexico was born. Spaniards married indigenous people, creating mestizo offspring—as well as a distinctive Mexican culture that was neither Spanish nor indigenous but combined elements of both.

Spain ruled Mexico for three centuries. After an unsuccessful revolution in 1810, Mexico finally won its independence in 1821.

But the newly born country continued to face many difficulties. Among them were bad rulers, beginning with a military officer named Agustín Iturbide, who had himself crowned emperor only a year after Mexico threw off the yoke of Spain. In 1848 Mexico lost a war with the United States—and was forced to give up almost half of its territory as a result. During the 1860s French forces invaded Mexico and installed a puppet emperor. While Mexico regained its independence in 1867 under national hero Benito Juárez, the long dictatorship of Porfirio Díaz would soon follow.

Díaz was overthrown in a revolution that began in 1910, but Mexico would be racked by fighting until the Partido Revolucionario Institucional took over in 1929. The PRI brought stability and economic progress, but its rule became increasingly corrupt.

Today, with the PRI's long monopoly on power swept away, Mexico stands on the brink of a new era. Difficult problems such as entrenched inequalities and grinding poverty remain. But progress toward a more open political system may lead to economic and social progress as well. Mexico—a land with a rich and ancient heritage—may emerge as one of the 21st century's most inspiring success stories.

1

THE OLMECS

From approximately 1150 B.C. to 400 B.C., the Olmecs were the ruling cultural group in what we now know as the United Mexican States. The Olmecs had a sophisticated culture. For instance, they were the first group of people in **Mesoamerica** known to have understood the concept of zero. They are believed to be the inventors of the first calendar used in Mesoamerica, and they are also thought to be responsible for the beginnings of the first Mesoamerican *hieroglyphic* writing system. The Olmecs are the oldest Mexican civilization archeologists have studied. Even so, much of Olmec life is a mystery.

Archeologists do know that the Olmecs lived along the central coast of the Gulf of Mexico, in an area due west of the Yucatán Peninsula. These people made their homes in the jungle river basins of modern-day Veracruz and Tabasco. As time passed, their numbers grew and their

The Olmecs created the earliest civilization in Mexico more than 3,000 years ago. The enormous stone heads they carved, such as this one at La Venta, are believed to have depicted important rulers. They may also have represented athletes, or even deities.

culture spread. Eventually, Olmec people lived throughout to the highlands of Mexico, the Valley of Mexico, Oaxaca, and parts of Guerrero.

San Lorenzo is the site of the oldest known Olmec cultural center, a city that existed from about 1150 B.C. to about 900 B.C. Archeologists believe it was a city for the elite or ruling class. Some historians think the city was destroyed when the **peasants** revolted. Others wonder if outsiders may have invaded it.

San Lorenzo is famous for its many ancient stone monuments. The most famous of these are the Olmec heads. The huge stone heads have large eyes and mouths, and their headgear appears to be that of warriors or perhaps rulers. Some people have even suggested that their hats look like the helmets of football players. If this **hypothesis** is true, then the stone heads may have been monuments to Olmec athletes.

The Olmec stone heads stand as tall as eight and a half feet tall. One stone head can weigh as much as 44 tons. These heads were carved from **basalt** and **jadeite**—without the use of metal tools!

The Olmecs made fine pottery and **jade** jewelry as well. They also carved figurines to represent their half-human, half-jaguar **deity**. The human-jaguar was an extremely important symbol in the Olmec culture. The Olmecs may have believed they were themselves descended from jaguars, and

The Olmecs have been called the "Rubber People" or the "People from the Land of Rubber." This is because they lived in an area that is known to produce a great deal of rubber. Several rubber balls were discovered at the Olmec site of El Manatí, near San Lorenzo. Archeologists believe that ball courts and rubber ball games were an important part of the Olmec culture.

In Mexican folklore, the jaguar is often associated with Tlaloc, the god of rain and fertility. These masks, recreations of masks created by the Olmecs, portray a hybrid between a jaguar and a human infant. The Olmec masks often showed the animal crying or snarling with an open mouth.

their **shamans** clearly held the jaguar in high regard. The Olmecs may have worshiped the human-jaguar as a combination fertility and rain god. They carved images of human-jaguars into their altar-like thrones. They also made masks in the image of the human-jaguar's face.

In Olmec artwork, human-jaguars look very young, more like chubby babies than adults. They were often given toothless sneers,

The stone remains of a tomb stand among other ruins at Villahermosa, the site of an ancient Olmec city.

and they sometimes had two large fangs. Their heads were misshapen and often had large splits in them. The human-jaguars seem to be neither male nor female.

The human-jaguar was not the only Olmec god. Archeologists have also found images of feathered serpents, harpy eagles, and sharks. The Olmecs probably worshiped all these animals. They may also have worshiped a fire god and a corn god.

Around 800 B.C., the Olmecs built the Great Pyramid at La Venta. It is only 100 feet tall, and compared to other Mesoamerican pyramids, it is actually quite small. The Mayans built much larger pyramids.

The sculpture on this Olmec altar depicts an important priest. The altar was found in the Olmec city at Villahermosa.

Olmec cultural centers seem to have been built in a very organized manner that was based on the people's spiritual beliefs. For instance, all the mounds at La Venta were built facing exactly eight degrees west of north. This may have been so that the Olmecs were always facing a certain star.

Archeologists can only guess about the reasons behind details like these, since the Olmecs did not leave real written histories of their culture. (Or if they did, archeologists have not found any of these records.) The Olmecs did, however, leave evidence of superior skills in math, timekeeping, agricultural irrigation, art, and jewelry making.

Their calendar shows a wide knowledge of astronomy, and their drainage systems are an example of early engineering skills.

The drainage systems found in the Olmec cities were underground arrangements of stone "pipelines." To create these drainage systems, the Olmecs pieced together U-shaped rectangular blocks of basalt and laid them end to end. The blocks were then covered with stones called capstones.

This 3,000-year-old slab of latex rubber may have been used by the Olmecs to play an ancient ball game. The game was probably similar to one played in later times throughout Mesoamerica. In this game, players tried to get a small rubber ball through a hoop, using their hips and shoulders. Ball games were a very important part of the Olmec culture, and losers may have been sacrificed to the gods.

Archeologists have suggested that these drainage systems were actually *aqueducts*. If this is true, the aqueducts may have been used to provide the Olmecs with fresh water. Monuments have been found in places along the underground pipe system of San Lorenzo that have led archeologists to believe the water systems also held religious meaning for the Olmecs.

Besides being skilled engineers, the Olmecs were farmers who grew corn, beans, and squash. And they were hunters as well as warriors. In Olmec artwork, many warriors are shown holding clubs.

The Olmecs' art and relics have led many scholars to call their civilization, "Mexico's Mother Culture." Other groups of people may have gone before them, but the Olmecs are the first Mesoamerican civilization to have left records of their rich architectural, scientific, agricultural, recreational, and artistic culture.

One of the most advanced ancient civilizations of Mexico was the Mayans.
Their civilization followed the Olmecs, flourishing more than 1,500 years ago.
This carving comes from the side of a Mayan building in Chichén Itzá, Yucatán.

2

THE MAYA

Much more is known about the Maya than about the Olmecs, because archeologists have found four Mayan books: the Dresden Codex, the Madrid Codex, the Paris Codex, and the Grolier Codex. Sadly, the humidity of the jungle is thought to have destroyed many other Mayan books. Spanish missionaries also destroyed many because they thought the books were evil.

The Mayan culture reached its highest point between the years A.D. 300 and 900. Mayan city-states covered the Yucatán Peninsula and reached as far south as the modern Mexican state of Chiapas and today's nations of Guatemala and Honduras.

The Mayan people were divided into classes: first the royalty; next, the priests; after the priests, the craftspeople and wealthy merchants; then the common people: fishermen, hunters, soldiers, farmers, and laborers; and last, the lowest members of Mayan society, the slaves.

The Mayan royalty included rulers and noblemen. The most important Mayan royal personage was the *Halach Uinic* ("True Man"). His position was handed down to him from his father or another male family member.

The rulers and priests lived in fine temples within the Mayan cities, while the noblemen lived in smaller houses also inside the city limits. The common people usually lived in much smaller homes outside the city.

The rulers and noblemen of the Mayan culture did not work. They depended on the working class and the slaves for their food, clothing, and other goods. All commoners were expected to respect and support the rulers, noblemen, and their priests.

The Mayan priests had their own hierarchy. The highest level a priest could reach was that of the *Ahau Kan Mai*. This priest led special religious ceremonies. The *Ahau Kan Mai* also taught the royal children.

The *Chilam* were the priests who led the daily religious ceremonies. They assisted the *Ahau Kan Mai* with his teaching chores. The *Chilam* priests went into trances and communicated with the Mayan gods. They were then expected to reveal the gods' messages to the other priests and the Mayan people. The *Chilam* priests were also doctors.

The *Nacon* were priests who led the people in sacrificial rituals. Their helpers were priests called *Chacs*, four old men named for the rain god. The *Chacs* were the ones who kept the sacrificial victims from moving when the *Nacon* cut the heart out of the victims' chests during religious rituals. The *Chacs* would each grasp a leg or an arm of the victim during the ceremony.

At Chichén Itzá there is a pyramid dedicated to Quetzalcoatl, the feathered serpent god. At the spring and winter equinoxes, the sun shines upon the pyramid's stairs and the serpent head at its base. The shadow creates the image of a snake that appears to slither down to earth from the sky. This is a good example of how the Maya aligned their ceremonial buildings with heavenly bodies for religious purposes.

The Mayan religion called for human sacrifices to feed the gods with blood. Mayan records indicate that captured enemy kings and warriors were the ones who were sacrificed at first, but later, prisoners, slaves, and children were used as sacrifices. Sometimes orphans and illegitimate children were purchased for use as victims.

The Maya had bloodletting ceremonies as well,

The ruins of major Mayan settlements have been found at Chichén Itzá and Uxmal, in the present-day Mexican state of Yucatán. This Mayan building in Uxmal is the Pyramid of Adivino.

where they pierced their bodies and tattooed themselves. This custom was apparently another part of their religious beliefs.

The Maya are also famous for their cities, pyramids, and palaces. These structures ranged from complicated palace buildings to temple-pyramids to simple thatched-roof huts. The palaces and temple-pyramids were often aligned with the sun, the moon, or the stars to honor the gods.

Mayan families lived in bungalows like this one on the Yucatán peninsula.

An advanced Mayan city was generally made up of a number of stepped platforms. The same type of platform formed the base for the temple-pyramids, palaces, and even some individual house mounds. All of these structures were centered around wide courtyards.

Pyramid-temples came in different sizes and shapes. Some Mayan pyramid-temples were high and extremely steep, while others were very wide or very short. They were different from Egyptian pyramids, because the Mayan pyramid-temples were built with flat platforms at their tops. Rulers and priests could gather here to overlook their people and their city.

The temples in the pyramids were not very big. The one to three rooms would have been very dark, lit only by torches or fires.

The inner chamber was the room in which the king and his priests performed the royal rituals. Often the temple exteriors were built to look like faces of great monsters or gods.

Some Mayan cities were surrounded by a moat. Others had stone or earthen walls built around them. These walls and moats may have been built toward the end of the Mayan reign when enemies began attacking Mayan cities.

The Maya were skilled farmers. They cleared large sections of tropical rain forest to use as farmlands. The method they used to clear the land of all trees is called the slash-and-burn method. First they cut down all the trees, and then they got rid of any other vegetation by burning. Finally, they planted their crops in the rich ashes left behind by the fires.

The Maya farmed squash, *maize*, beans, chilies, avocado, papaya, guava, watermelon, cantaloupe, tomatoes, sweet potatoes, and plums. They traded crops like cotton, tobacco, palm oil, salt, and *cacao*. To trade, the Maya set up road systems between neighboring cities and cultural centers.

These people worked hard to meet their standards for physical beauty. They decorated their bodies with paint and tattoos, and they wore colorful clothing and hats that revealed their social status. The bigger and more ornate the hat, the more important the individual was. Teeth were also an important aspect of beauty in their culture. The Maya filed

According to legend, a magic dwarf built the Pyramid of the Magician in one night and then took control of the city. The pyramid in Uxmal is also called *Casa del Enano*—the House of the Dwarf.

their teeth until they were very pointed or T-shaped. They decorated their teeth with **pyrite, obsidian**, or jade. Their noses, ears, and lips were often pierced and adorned with jewelry made from jade, shells, and other natural materials.

But the Maya also took even more extreme measures to achieve their concept of beauty. Mayan mothers tied their newborn infants' heads between two boards for several days. This created enough pressure to make the skull permanently longer with a backward slope. Archeologists think that the Maya did this to try and make their children's heads resemble ears of corn, since the corn god's head was often portrayed as long and narrow with a cornhusk attached to it. Corn was the mainstay of the Mayan diet, and the corn god was important to them.

The Maya believed being cross-eyed was a good thing. To try to make her child cross-eyed, a Mayan mother would hang a small bright object between her child's eyes, hoping that if the child looked at this object long enough, the eyes would become permanently crossed. This practice is still carried out by some Mayan mothers today.

In 1952, a tomb in a pyramid-temple at Palenque was opened. The tomb belonged to a Mayan king named Pacal. The opening of Pacal's tomb proved that Mayan pyramids were used as burial vaults. Up until then, most people believed that they were merely the bases for Mayan temples.

Pacal was the son and grandson of two unusual rulers. His mother and grandmother were powerful female rulers. Mayan kings were traditionally the descendants of kings, but Pacal's father was not a king. Pacal had to silence the people who thought he should not be king, so he told the people that his mother was the Mother Goddess. In the eyes of his people, Pacal was a direct descendent of the gods.

A carved figure from the temple of Quetzalcoatl, in the ancient Mayan city of Teotihuacán. Quetzalcoatl was an important and powerful deity who was believed to have taught the people of Mexico how to grow crops.

Time was another important concept to the Maya. They used two different types of dating systems, and the Calendar Round is a combination of these two methods. One dating system is based on a 260-day cycle; the other is based on a year of 365 days. The Calendar Round starts a new "century" every 52 years. The Long Count is a linear count of days since a mythical Zero Date, or starting point. The Maya believed that this date was equivalent to the year 3314 B.C. The

Today the Mayan ruins at Uxmal draw thousands of tourists, who are interested in the ancient civilizations of Mexico.

Mayan calendar has survived time, jungle humidity, and Spanish invaders. Its accuracy amazes scholars.

The Maya also had a highly developed numerical system composed of bars and dots that were combined to symbolize numbers. The base of the Mayan number system was 20, and the Maya wrote numbers larger than 19 in powers of 20. A dot stood for one in this system, and a bar symbolized five. Numbers were written from the bottom up.

Today, the Mayan people still survive. Many continue to live on the Yucatán Peninsula of Mexico. Here, Mayan women can still be seen wearing *huipils* (wee-peels), the traditional embroidered cotton shirts. The embroidery and weaving designs can be traced back to the Maya's ancient ancestors. The *huipils* silently offer information about the wearer's village, her social and marital status, religious background, wealth, power, and personality.

Huipils are not the only thing modern-day Maya have in common with their ancestors. The Mayan language is still alive in remote areas of Mexico, and slash-and-burn farming is still practiced. Many Mayan foods and customs remain the same as well.

The ancient Maya were an ingenious culture. Their buildings and scientific achievements grew out of foundation left by the Olmecs. Today, many archeologists and anthropologists believe that the Mayan civilization was the most advanced of all the Mesoamerican cultures.

3

THE AZTECS

The Aztecs told their Spanish conquerors they were descended from an earlier people, the Toltecs. By the time the Aztecs had reached the Valley of Mexico some 300 years earlier, the Toltecs were no longer a powerful force there. Instead, when the Aztecs migrated to the Valley of Mexico from the north around A.D. 1200, the Tepanecs were one of the ruling tribes. The more numerous Tepanecs bullied the Aztecs and pushed them away from the best farmlands. At one point, the powerful Tepanecs may even have enslaved the Aztecs. The fierce Aztec warriors probably served as mercenary soldiers for the stronger society.

The Aztecs would not be dominated for long, however. They continued to wander, until they found a place in the Valley of Mexico, a site they believed fulfilled a prophesy for their people.

This mural on a wall of the Palacio Nacional in Mexico City depicts Aztec life. The Aztecs are probably the most famous of Mexico's ancient civilizations, but their influence and importance lasted a relatively short time. Although they controlled an empire that covered much of Mexico during the 14th and early 15th centuries, by the 1520s the Spanish had shattered their power.

30

They claimed an island in the middle of Lake Texcoco sometime around A.D. 1325, where they built the city of Tenochtitlán. Here they settled and grew stronger.

Their religion ruled their lives. It was a religion that featured many gods and called for many human sacrifices. The Aztecs built great monuments to their god. For example, Tenochtitlán's main ceremonial buildings were built in honor of the Sun and War God (Huitzilopochtli), the Rain God (Tlaloc), and Quetzalcoatl, the Feathered Serpent.

The Aztecs soon conquered the other tribes of the Valley. The Aztecs became famous for their military intelligence and strength. They also became legendary for their human sacrifices.

Aztec sacrificial rituals were timed according to their calendar. Every month of their calendar had at least one festival to honor one of their many gods. During these festivals, the people would honor a specific god with ritual music, traditional dances, parades, and sacrifices. Aztec sacrificial ceremonies were important events. The priests, king and queen, nobility, and warriors all gathered for the ceremonies. The people of the surrounding town would be called to watch as well. The priests' job was to keep track of the rituals, the sacrifices, and the calendar.

The Aztecs believed that in

Legend says the Aztecs saw what they believed was an omen telling them where to build their great city. The sign was an eagle perched on a cactus. The eagle had a serpent in his talons. This symbol is now featured on the Mexican flag.

The Aztecs called themselves the Mexica, from which comes the nation's name today. Today, Mexico's national capital, Mexico City, stands tall above the ancient ruins of Tenochtitlán, the city built by the mighty Aztecs long ago in the Valley of Mexico.

The Toltecs were one of several native groups living in the Valley of Mexico during the 14th century. These Toltec statues are part of a complex at Tula, in the present-day state of Hidalgo.

order to keep their gods strong, they had to supply them with human blood. The Aztec kings and queens often participated in bloodletting rituals, offering their own blood to strengthen their gods. They believed that if they kept their gods strong, then the gods would protect them.

The Aztec city of Tenochtitlán became the cultural and military capital of the Valley of Mexico. The population of the city probably

The religion of the Aztecs was bloody and brutal, as illustrated by this drawing from an ancient codex. A priest is holding the bleeding heart of a sacrifice victim aloft to the god Huitzilopochtli. Another victim lies at the foot of the altar. The Aztecs believed Huitzilopochtli, the sun god, needed sacrifices of human blood in order to climb into the sky to start each new day. Without regular sacrifice, the sun would not rise and the world would end.

reached close to 100,000 inhabitants. The Aztecs prospered in their swampy homeland.

One reason that the Aztecs flourished was their unique way of farming. Before they gained control of the Mexico Valley area, the

Aztecs had been forced away from good farming lands by stronger tribes like the Tepanec. The ingenious Aztecs learned how to make the best of a bad situation. They created their own farmland in the midst of the swamps of Tenochtitlán.

The Aztecs created floating gardens called *chinampas*, used to grow vegetables, flowers, and trees. First, they built a raft out of rushes and reeds. Next, mud was piled onto the raft, and the mud was seeded or plants were transplanted into it. Finally, the plants were given time to grow on the *chinampas*. The plant roots grew through the rafts down to the water. Special trees were planted that would grow strong roots attached to the lake bottom. The plants watered themselves, while the trees anchored the rafts in place. Sometimes *chinampas* were tied together to create large, anchored islands. Some archeologists believe some were roomy enough to put gardeners' huts on them.

Even after the Aztecs gained control of the land, they continued to use their floating gardens. These gardens were particularly fertile because much of the mud used came from the lake bottom. The lake bottom would have been rich in nutrients from fish and plants that had decomposed there.

Tenochtitlán became a major center for traders. The market was filled with fruits, vegetables, flowers, clothing, pottery, and craft items. Metal craftsmen traded their wares during market

When the Aztecs performed human sacrifices, the victim was taken to the top of a ceremonial pyramid-temple, where he or she was lifted onto an altar. Next, an Aztec priest would cut out the victim's heart. The heart was lifted up toward the sky in a gesture of offering to whatever god was being worshiped on that occasion. Finally, the heart was thrown into a ceremonial fire.

33

time. They made jewelry and other items from copper, gold, and silver. The Aztecs did not use money. Instead, they bartered for most goods and services.

One Aztec product was a chocolate drink made from the beans of the cacao tree. They used the cacao beans for flavoring foods. They also probably made candies from the beans.

The Aztecs had two sides to their nature. On the one hand, they were a very agricultural people. They loved flowers and the land. They farmed their *chinampas* and farmlands, and they grew corn, beans, and other food. On the other hand, though, they were a military society. They were cunning warriors who are believed to have slaughtered tens of thousands of their prisoners as human sacrifices.

A **hereditary** emperor supported by the military and priests ruled the common people. The commoners were forced to supply the imperial family, the military, and the priests with food, clothing, and shelter. The Aztec military maintained order through swift and often brutal punishment for disobedience. Oddly enough, the Aztecs' most famous king welcomed the Spanish. His actions soon lead to the downfall of the Aztec empire.

Montezuma (1480–1520) was the Aztec king who opened his empire to the Spanish empire. His decision was based on superstitions and prophecies. The great king believed that the European men on horses were gods and that their arrival fulfilled an ancient prophecy.

The Aztecs often sacrificed slaves or prisoners captured in battle. Weaker tribes also had to send sacrificial victims each year as tribute. Sometimes the Aztecs sacrificed children.

The Sun Stone, an Aztec calendar, was salvaged from Tenochtitlán. It is considered one of the most important artifacts displayed at the Museo Nacional de Antropología (National Museum of Anthropology) in Mexico City.

Montezuma thought Hernán Cortés was the descendent of the god Quetzalcoatl, who, according to legend, had left Mexico in the 10th century. The prophecy went on to say that the god would return from the east to recover his power over the Aztecs. Montezuma and his people believed that Cortés's arrival was the fulfillment of this prophecy. In many ways, these beliefs were the undoing of the great Aztec empire. Montezuma gave the Spaniards gold, cacao beans,

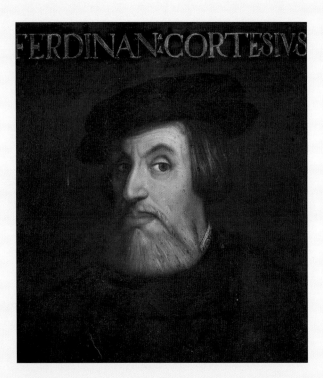

One of the most important events in Mexico's history was the arrival of the Spanish conquistador Hernán Cortés in 1519. With a small army Cortés conquered the mighty Aztec empire and took control of the region, which became known as New Spain. The blending of native and Spanish cultures produced Mexico's modern mestizo culture.

clothing, and other gifts. Unfortunately for Montezuma and the Aztecs, however, interactions between the Spaniards and the Aztecs soon became tense.

Cortés took Montezuma prisoner. When the Aztecs began to revolt, Cortés ordered Montezuma to tell the people to stop. When Montezuma complied with Cortés' orders, an angry member of the mob struck Montezuma in the head with a stone. The Aztec ruler died three days later.

Cortés retreated to Tlaxcalan territory. He lost many soldiers on the way, but the Spanish returned to besiege Tenochtitlán in 1521 with an army of native Aztecs at their side. The Spanish and their allies cut the city off from the outside world. Tenochtitlán's inhabitants could not trade with outsiders, receive food, or fresh water. *Smallpox* afflicted the Aztecs and further diminished their strength.

At last, Cortés entered the city with his troops. He destroyed temples, homes, and palaces. With the fall of the Aztec buildings, came the final fall of their empire's hold on Mesoamerica.

Shortly after their victory, Cortés and his men began building a European-style city atop the ruins of Tenochtitlán. By 1540, Mexico City was the new central city of Spanish America. As Spanish control spread throughout Mesoamerica, Mexico would never be the same.

IN THE CONQUEST OF NEW SPAIN, BERNAL DÍAZ DEL CASTILLIO, SOLDIER TO CORTÉS, WRITES:

When we came near to Mexico, at a place where there where some other small towers, the Great Montezuma descended from his litter, and these other great Caciques support him beneath a marvelously rich canopy of green feathers, decorated with gold work, silver, pearls, and chalchihuites, which hung from a sort of border. It was a marvelous site. The Great Montezuma was magnificently clad, in their fashion, and wore sandals of a kind for which their name is cactli, the soles of which are of gold and the upper parts ornamented with precious stones. And the four other lords who supported him where richly clad also in garments that seemed to have been kept ready for them on the road so that they would accompany their master. For they had not worn clothes like this when they came out to receive us. The were four other great Caciques who carried the canopy above their heads, and many more lords who walked before the great Montezuma, sweeping the ground on which he was to tread, and laying down cloaks so that his feet should not touch the earth. Not one of these chieftains dared to look him in the face. All kept their eyes lowered most reverently except those four lords, his nephews, who were supporting him.

These Tarahumara Indian girls are wearing traditional dresses. The Tarahumara are descended from natives of Mexico. Most live in the Sierra Madre Mountains apart from Mexico's *mestizo* civilization.

MESTIZOS, CRIOLLOS, MULATTOS, AND INDIGENOUS MEXICANS

Mestizos, from a Spanish word that means "mixed," have both Spanish—or European—and Native American ancestry. The first generations of Mexican *mestizos* were the children of Spanish fathers and Indian mothers. At first, *mestizos* occupied a social status that was higher socially than the Indians but lower than the pureblood Spaniards.

Things have greatly changed, however. Now, *mestizos* are the largest social group in Mexico. Today, *mestizos* are proud of their mixed heritage, and many of Mexico's famous citizens are of *mestizo* descent.

Unlike *mestizos*, *criollos* were people of pure Spanish descent who were born in New Spain (what is now Mexico). By the early 19th century, these people grew tired of paying higher and higher taxes to Spain, and Mexico's 11 years of rebellion and revolution were started, organized, and supported by the *criollos*. After Mexico gained its independence from Spain in 1821, for many years the *criollos* were the ruling class of Mexico. Today, in Mexico the word *criollo* is also used to describe the small population of American, Canadian, and European people living there.

Mulattos are yet another group of Mexicans, a mixture of African ancestry with Indian or *mestizo*. During the 17th and 18th centuries, the Spanish and European settlers brought African slaves to New Spain. Some of these slaves married Indians or *mestizos*. Their children were the first generation of mulattos in Mexico.

The Tarahumara people are an **indigenous** group of Native Americans. A number of these people live in the Sierra Madres of northwest Chihuahua. The Tarahumara people retreated into the mountains when the Spanish invaded Mexico. Some of them have continued living in relative isolation in an attempt to maintain their traditional language and lifestyle.

This tribe of people, known throughout Mexico as the Tarahumara, call themselves the Rarámuri people. This means "people who are light of foot." They are known to be excellent long-distance runners. Some have run as far as 100 miles non-stop! They love to have races among themselves, and they run up and down the sides of steep mountains, just for fun. The Tarahumara people are such good runners that they often hunt deer by chasing them until the deer grow too tired to run.

A Tarahumara game is called the *rarahipa*. It is a type of kickball race that involves two teams. The members of the team kick a wooden

A Seri Indian woman sports a traditional Mexican head wrap. Many of the native people of Mexico continue to follow the customs of their culture.

ball as they run. The game often lasts all day and all night.

The traditional Tarahumara people live in caves during the winter and in wooden huts during the summers. They farm the land and raise cattle, sheep, and goats. They are also known for making a corn beer called *tesgüino*. The women weave cloth from wool on homemade looms.

The Seri are yet another indigenous people. They live in the villages of Punta Chueca and El Desemboque, which have a combined population of somewhere between 600 and 800. Only about 200 of these people are full-blooded Seri; the other 400 to 600 people are a mixture of Seri and *mestizo* or other bloodlines.

The Seri call themselves the Konkaak, which simply means "the People." They are a tall, slim people with very dark skin and bright

A Mexican shaman sits in a *temazcal*—a sauna designed to heal illness and discomfort. Shamans, or priests, play a very important role in the lives of the Cora Indians, who live in the Nayarit region of Mexico.

eyes. They eke out a living from fishing, basket weaving, and woodcarving. The women make fine baskets and the men specialize in ironwood carvings. The traditional Seri people still sleep outside under the night stars. Most sleep right on the ground, with only a blanket for cover. They are extremely poor.

Traditionally, Seri women and men painted their faces. A Seri could tell a married woman from a single woman by her face paints. Often, the Seri medicine men suggested face painting as a sort of spiritual protection for their people. Now, though, this is a dying art, reserved for special events only.

Like the Seri, the Cora live a traditional lifestyle. Only a few thousand full-blooded Cora remain in modern-day Mexico. They live in the state of Nayarit in western Mexico. There they farm, raise cattle, and produce beautiful woven textiles. They grow corn, beans, squash, and cucumbers on steep hillsides. These people eat very little meat, but sometimes they own a cow or goat for milk and cheese.

The Cora Indians are recognized as skilled mask makers. They still celebrate *fiestas* by wearing masks and painting their bodies. Their masks are made out of papier-maché, feathers, fur, wool, wood, and other materials. Some masks are ugly, while others are comical. Some are of animal faces and others portray human faces.

The Cora's closest neighbors are the Wixarica (wee-sha-ree-ka). Most of these people live in the Jalisco and Nayarit regions. Their language is very close to the ancient language of the Aztecs. Their mountainous homeland is very harsh, and their crops are often lost to poor soil and extreme weather conditions. Often, the Wixarica pray for rain.

These people's shamans are important to their daily lives. The shamans, called *Marakame*, perform ritual ceremonies to ask the gods for help with their crops. For instance, in one ceremony, the priests ingest *peyote*. First, however, the Marakame must make a pilgrimage to Wirikuta to get this potent *hallucinogen*. The Marakame then sacrifice deer. Finally, they cover corn with the deer blood. The ceremony has direct ties to pre-Columbian rituals of the Wixarica's ancestors.

The Wixarica are talented artists who depend on tourists to buy crafts. The Wixarica enjoy working with beeswax, glass beads, and wood. They love to use bright colors and bold patterns in their work.

If they cannot sell their artwork and exist on the income it produces, many Wixarica work in the tobacco fields of their region.

The Tarascan Indians can be found in northern Michoacán and along the shores of Lake Patzcuaro. Some researchers believe they are descendants of an ancient Peruvian tribe of Indians. Today, they are a strong community, with more than 80,000 members. The Tarascan have retained their native language and traditions.

These Indians are skilled artisans who make pottery, guitars, furniture, copperware, leather goods, textiles, and wooden masks. Almost every Tarascan village has its own special craft. Paracho is a village that is famous for its guitars, while Santa Clara is known for its copperware.

Another indigenous group, the Totonacs, live along the lush coastlands of Veracruz and in the highlands of the Sierra Madre. As many as 150,000 of these people are estimated to be living in Mexico today. Although they have technically been converted to Catholicism, the Totonacs practice a religion that is a mixture of pre-Columbian and Catholic rituals.

This tribe has been pushed off its homelands by the growth of cattle farming, recent oil discoveries in the Gulf of Mexico, and the expansion of already large vanilla, tobacco, sugar cane, and coffee farms. As a result, the Totonacs have begun, like many other indigenous peoples of Mexico, to depend on tourism for their living.

The Totonacs survive on a diet that consists mainly of corn, beans, and chilies. Vegetables, wild roots, and other plants round out their simple menu. They generally slaughter their domestic animals, such as cows and chickens, only during fiestas.

A group of Mayans known as the Papantla Flyers performs at Tulum, Quintana Roo. They are reenacting an ancient Totonac ceremony intended to bring rain for farmers.

During these fiestas the Totonacs are famous for performing their *Danza de los Voladores* (Dance of the Fliers). They now expect tourists to pay for the honor of witnessing this event. Five men, dressed in ornate bird-like costumes, perform the dance by climbing atop a tall pole. One stands in the center of a small platform and plays a traditional reed flute and drum. The others tie themselves to the pole with ropes attached to one of their legs. They then

A statue of a Spanish missionary is silhouetted against the dusky sky in Querétaro City. Although there are still many Amerindian people living in Mexico, the great majority of the population is *mestizo* and Spanish influences permeate the culture.

push themselves backward off the platform and revolve around the pole 13 times, until they reach the ground.

Although in pre-Columbian times this was a highly sacred fertility ritual, now the dance has been reduced to a mere tourist-pleasing dance performance. The Totonacs perform this dance at the ruins of El Tajín and at the Museum of Anthropology in Mexico City. The dance has become the source of livelihood for many Totonacs.

Still more indigenous groups, the Tzotzils and Tzeltals, live in the Chiapas highland area surrounding San Cristóbal de las Casas. The native language of both of these tribes is a Mayan dialect. The Tzotzils live on the upper slopes of the Central Mountains, above the 5,000-foot elevation level. The Tzeltals live on the lower slopes of the Central Mountains.

The Tzotzils are an agricultural people. They farm corn, beans, and squash. They use the slash-and-burn farming technique used by many indigenous Mexicans. The Tzotzils also use hoes and digging sticks to cultivate their fields. Peaches are their most important crop, and they raise sheep for wool for weaving. Tzotzil women also make pottery.

The Tzeltal Indians are an agricultural people as well. They grow beans, chilies, and corn, using the same farming methods as their neighbors, the Tzotzils. Both tribes often sell their crops at the markets of San Cristóbal de las Casas. Both tribes live in houses made of logs with thatched roofs.

Both tribes also tend to dress in traditional clothing. The styles differ only slightly from area to area. The men wear short pants with knee-length shirts. Most wear hats, sandals, and a sash, also. The colors of the clothing usually vary from community to community. The women of both tribes wear long wraparound skirts made out of wool. They also wear sashes, cotton blouses or tunics, and **rebozos**. Women do not generally wear shoes.

The diverse heritages of all these Mexican people add to their nation's cultural strength. Together, *mestizos*, *criollos*, mulattos, and indigenous Mexicans make Mexico a unique and beautiful nation.

LIFE IN MEXICO TODAY

Today about four out of every five Mexicans live in an urban area of their nation. Mexicans who live in these cities work at many of the same types of jobs that Americans do: they are teachers, lawyers, doctors, and factory workers.

Nearly a half of Mexico's working population is employed by *service industries*. Another quarter of the population is employed in some other sort of industrial pursuit. The main industries in Mexico are the food and beverage industry, tobacco production, iron and steel manufacturing, clothing fabrication, automobile production, and the tourism industry. The final quarter of the population works on farms.

Mexico's urban population has boomed over the last 50 years or so. This has created problems such as overcrowding, high levels of pollution, and an increase in Mexico's homeless population. The

A view of crowded Guanajuato City. Today, almost 80 percent of Mexicans live in or near cities. Mexico City, which has about 20 million people living in and around the city, is the largest city in Mexico and one of the largest in the world.

Mexican government is working diligently to try and find solutions for these problems.

Many Mexicans who work on farms live on *ejidos*. An ejido is a farm owned by a group of Mexican families. It may be run as a group effort or divided into separate plots for each of the families to work on their own. Over half of Mexico's farmers own land under the ejido system.

The homes of most ejido farmers are small, **adobe** buildings. They do not have electricity or running water. Family members rarely even have beds to sleep on at night. The floors are usually dirt, and at night, straw mats called *petates* are put on the floor.

Many other Mexicans live in villages. These small towns almost always have a plaza, or village square, and a marketplace. The plaza is used for fiestas, celebrations, and community gatherings. The marketplace is a colorful trade center where people come to barter, trade, and sell fruits, vegetables, artworks, handicrafts, balloons, specialty foods, and clothing.

Spanish is the official language of Mexico, but at least 50 native languages are still spoken in the rural communities of Mexico. In order to get better jobs, many people from the more rural areas are making an effort to learn Spanish. They

A favorite Mexican dish often eaten at fiestas is called *esquites*. To make this dish you will need 6 tender ears of corn, half a bar of butter, 3 lemons, ground chili to sprinkle on top, and salt.

Once you have gathered these ingredients, you will have to:

1. Remove the kernels of corn from the cob.
2. Melt butter in a sauce pan and add the corn.
3. Cook slowly, gradually adding water and salt.

Before serving, sprinkle some chili over the top and add lemon juice to taste. You can also add mayonnaise or cheese.
Now...enjoy!

A community of peers is a vital source of support for Mexican farmers. The members of an ejido, or farming collective, sit in a large circle at a meeting.

are encouraging their children to learn Spanish as well. This way, they will be more able to survive in Mexico's rapidly growing urban areas.

Whether they live in urban or rural areas, all Mexican children between the ages of six and 16 must attend school. Children attend *primaria*, or primary school, from the ages of six to 12. At 13, they begin their *secundaria*, or high school. After three years of high school, they may attend four years of *preparatoria*, which is preparation for college.

The Mexican government spends a great deal of money on its educational system. Children are expected to be on their best behavior

A Tarahumara girl sells crafts to tourists. Mexico has become a favorite destination for foreign visitors, who contribute millions of dollars each year to the country's economy. Even those who do not directly work in tourism-related service industries benefit from tourism.

when they are in school. They learn about history, mathematics, science, literature, dance, the arts, and geography.

After students attend *preparatoria*, they can go on to college. There are over 300 schools of higher learning in Mexico. Some of these schools are trade schools; others are universities. A few colleges are dedicated specifically to training future teachers.

No matter how much or how little education Mexicans have, their family life is very important. Whether the family lives in the rural regions of the country or the more modern urban centers, extended family members living together are not unusual. Most Mexican families are deeply religious and close knit. They are predominantly Roman Catholic.

The traditional Mexican mother cooks, cleans, and cares for the children. The father is usually the one who works outside the home. He is also, traditionally, the one who is considered the head of the household.

Machismo is an important concept to Mexican men, one that is sometimes hard for others to understand. It has to do with the bold, aggressive nature of men, but it is more than that. Machismo is also a sense that men are responsible for the protection of their families. They are the authority figures in the family.

Mexican children are expected to be respectful, polite, and well behaved. They are taught to respect and listen to their elders. Oftentimes, grandparents have a large role in children's upbringings.

Although most Mexicans share these common family values, Mexican clothing is as diverse as that of Americans. Rural Indians still dress in the traditional clothing of their ancestors, while well-to-do modern young people dress in blue jeans and t-shirts. Other Mexicans dress in skirts and blouses or *charros* (the bright costumes of the Mexican bullfighters), and some Mexicans still wear **sombreros**. Others, however, now prefer to wear baseball hats or bandannas on their heads.

But although they may dress differently, all Mexicans love their fiestas. Each year, more than 5,000 fiestas take place in Mexico. Some are official and others are personal, religious, or food fiestas and *ferias* (street fairs).

Another form of entertainment in Mexico is soccer—but Mexicans call this sport *fútbol*. Baseball, or *béisbol*, is a very popular sport as well. Mexicans also love jai alai, a game that was brought to their country from Spain.

In jai alai, a *cesta*, or wicker bat, is tied to the players' wrists. The players hit a hard rubber ball called a *pelota*. The rules of jai alai are a lot like those of tennis and racquetball. All games start with a serve, which must land in a certain area of the jai alai court. The receiving player has to catch the pelota in the air or on the first bounce, then get it back to the wall in one continuous motion. The players continue to lob the pelota back and forth, until the pelota is missed or goes out of bounds.

Bullfights are another favorite form of entertainment that was brought over from Spain. Mexico has more than 200 bullfighting arenas, and the season lasts from November to April. Tourists and Mexican citizens alike flock to watch these events.

Matadors are master bullfighters. They wear elaborate costumes, called "suits of lights" because they are covered with silver and gold sequins that shine in the sunlight. Great matadors are honored heroes in Mexico.

Soccer, known as *fútbol*, is one of the most popular sports in Mexico today. The sport is believed to have originated in Mexico, as the Mayans were known to have played a game with similar rules.

Although Mexicans love to have a good time, many Mexicans suffer from poverty and poor living conditions. Super Barrio is a relatively new phenomenon that seeks to battle these conditions.

On June 12, 1987, a group of people had gathered to protest poor housing conditions. Suddenly, a masked figure appeared in a flurry of fireworks. He was wearing red tights and a yellow cape, with the letters SB emblazoned on his chest. Since that day, Super Barrio has fought for the rights of the poor, elderly, homeless, hungry, and weak. The character of Super Barrio is believed to be played by not one but many men. All of these men work together to combat pollution, poor

A man walks past sacks of grain outside a hardware store in Oaxaca. As Mexico continues to take steps toward solving its social and economic problems, the future looks bright for Mexicans of all backgrounds.

housing conditions, abuse of the elderly, and much more.

Super Barrio is just one example of Mexican strength and creativity. In the past, Mexicans have withstood invasions, revolutions, and droughts; in recent times, they have survived earthquakes, volcanic eruptions, and changing government leadership. They have managed to retain the best of their native ancestors' traditions and combined it with the best of their Spanish forefathers' heritage. No matter what, the Mexican spirit seems to rise above the problems of the nation.

Today the government and people of Mexico are working together to stop pollution, overpopulation, and drug trafficking. Measures are being taken to prevent the depletion of the rainforests. Government money is being poured into the educational system to help train Mexico's young for the future.

The people of Mexico are resilient and artistic. They face many social problems—but their strong faith, deep family ties, and rich creativity will help them move forward with pride into the 21st century.

58

CHRONOLOGY

1150–400 B.C.	Rise and fall of Olmec Civilization; Mayans begin rise.
A.D. 300–900	Peak of Mayan culture.
1325	Aztecs found the city of Tenochtitlán.
1519-1521	Spanish invasion and conquest of Mexico.
1521-1821	Spanish colonial era.
1910-1921	Mexican Revolution.
1929	The first formal Mexican political party is born. It is called the National Revolutionary Party. It is now the Party Revolutionary Institutional, or the PRI.
1985	Earthquake hits Mexico City. Thousands of people are killed.
1994	North America Free Trade Agreement (NAFTA) between Canada, the United States, and Mexico goes into effect.
2001	President Fox meets with U.S. President George W. Bush to discuss a cooperative relationship between the neighboring countries.
2003	Congressional elections have an unusually low voter turnout; no political party gains a clear majority in Congress.
2006	An Aztec altar and massive stone slab, each over 500 years old, are discovered in Mexico City; Felipe Calderón is elected president amidst allegations of voter fraud.
2007	Archaeologists discover the remains of a 2,500-year-old, Olmec-influenced city in central Mexico.
2008	Despite the efforts of Mexican law enforcement agencies, drug-related gang violence remains a major problem in many parts of the country.

FURTHER READING

Chávez, Alicia Hernández. *Mexico: A Brief History*. Berkeley: University of California Press, 2006.

Coe, Michael D., and Rex Koontz. *Mexico: From the Olmecs to the Aztecs*. New York: Thames and Hudson, 2008.

Franz, Carl, et al. *The People's Guide to Mexico*. Berkeley, Calif.: Avalon Travel Publishing, 2006.

Hamnet, Brian R. *A Concise History of Mexico*. New York: Cambridge University Press, 2006.

Joseph, Gilbert M., editor. *The Mexico Reader: History, Culture, Politics*. Durham, N.C.: Duke University Press, 2002.

Kalman, Bobbie. *Mexico: The People*. New York: Crabtree, 2008.

Levy, Daniel C., and Kathleen Bruhn. *Mexico: The Struggle for Democratic Development*. Berkeley: University of California Press, 2006.

Mayor, Guy. *Mexico: A Quick Guide to Customs and Etiquette*. New York: Kuperard, 2006.

Meyer, Michael C., et al. *The Course of Mexican History*. New York: Oxford University Press, 2002.

Peterson, Joan. *Eat Smart in Mexico*. Corte Madera: Ginko Press, 2008.

INTERNET RESOURCES

Indigenous Peoples of Mexico
http://www.indians.org/welker/mexmain2.htm

Mexican Heritage
http://www.angelfire.com/ca5/mexhistory/

Mexico Connect
http://www.mexconnect.com

Mexico Online
http://www.mexonline.com/history.htm

Mexico People
https://www.cia.gov/library/publications/the-world-factbook/geos/mx.html

Mexico Reference Desk
http://lanic.utexas.edu/la/Mexico

GLOSSARY

Adobe	A building material made of mud and straw.
Aqueducts	Systems of pipes meant to carry running water.
Basalt	A dark, dense rock produced by volcanoes.
Cacao	The bean from which chocolate is made.
Deity	A god.
Fiestas	Spanish parties or holidays.
Hallucinogen	A drug that causes you to perceive things that are not really there.
Hereditary	Passed down from generation to generation.
Hieroglyphic	Written in a system of pictures.
Hypothesis	A theory.
Indigenous	Native to a certain area.
Jade	A green stone.
Jadeite	A kind of jade.
Maize	Indian corn.
Mesoamerica	The region of southern North America that was inhabited before the arrival of the Spaniards.
Obsidian	A dark natural glass formed by the cooling of molten lava.
Peasants	Common people.
Peyote	A drug from the mescal cactus that causes hallucinations.
Pyrite	A yellow metal, also called fool's gold.
Rebozos	A long scarf worn by Mexican women.
Service industries	Organizations that provide services to the community, such as hospitals, restaurants, waste collection, etc.
Shamans	Holy men or priests.
Smallpox	A contagious disease that causes high fevers and pus-filled sores that leave deep scars.
Sombreros	Wide-brimmed, Mexican hats made of felt or straw.

INDEX

62

63

PICTURE CREDITS

CONTRIBUTORS

Roger E. Hernández is the most widely syndicated columnist writing on Hispanic issues in the United States. His weekly column, distributed by King Features, appears in some 40 newspapers across the country, including the *Washington Post*, *Los Angeles Daily News*, *Dallas Morning News*, *Arizona Republic*, *Rocky Mountain News* in Denver, *El Paso Times*, and *Hartford Courant*. He is also the author of *Cubans in America*, an illustrated history of the Cuban presence in what is now the United States, from the early colonists in 16th-century Florida to today's Castro-era exiles. The book was designed to accompany a PBS documentary of the same title.

Hernández's articles and essays have been published in the *New York Times*, *New Jersey Monthly*, *Reader's Digest*, and *Vista Magazine*; he is a frequent guest on television and radio political talk shows, and often travels the country to lecture on his topic of expertise. Currently, he is teaching journalism and English composition at the New Jersey Institute of Technology in Newark, where he holds the position of writer-in-residence. He is also a member of the adjunct faculty at Rutgers University.

Hernández left Cuba with his parents at the age of nine. After living in Spain for a year, the family settled in Union City, New Jersey, where Hernández grew up. He attended Rutgers University, where he earned a BA in Journalism in 1977; after graduation, he worked in television news before moving to print journalism in 1983. He lives with his wife and two children in Upper Montclair, New Jersey.

AUTHOR

Colleen Madonna Flood Williams holds a bachelor's degree in elementary education, with a minor in art. She is the author of numerous study units, magazine articles, newspaper articles, essays, and poems. Colleen lives in Soldotna, Alaska, with her husband Paul, her son Dillon, and their Bouvier des Flandres dog, Kosmos Kramer.